THE EDUCATION OF CHILDREN FROM THE STANDPOINT OF THEOSOPHY

THE EDUCATION
OF CHILDREN
FROM THE
STANDPOINT OF
THEOSOPHY

RUDOLPH STEINER

Contents

TWENTY-FIRST CENTURY EDITION, USA

It is necessary, I think, to celebrate the women whose work moved within and sometimes beyond the margins of Theosophy—who did not always name what they were doing as spiritual, but who understood, intuitively or otherwise, that geometry is sacred and that color speaks. Hilma af Klint painted her spirals and cosmograms in the early 1900s, before abstraction had an audience, let alone a language. Emma Kunz worked with pendulums and graph paper to suggest science but point elsewhere. Agnes Pelton gave desert silence a palette. These women were not decorating philosophy; they were drafting alternative systems of thinking in oil, gouache, graphite. Today, their influence is being re-read, not as footnote but as an architecture—work that laid out structures we didn't yet have the names for. I follow in their wake, using installation, textiles, and digital forms to test the edges of intuition. What we share is not a belief system, necessarily, but a sensibility: the idea that some truths have to be triangulated by shape and poetry, that color can offer what language won't, and that a line, properly set, can carry intention like an electric current, unforgettable, crystalline, immediate.

-LC

Rudolph Steiner

Rudolf Steiner

A brilliant architect of Education for a World Obsessed With Measuring Success

In the era of superdata, where algorithms govern not only our daily choices but increasingly the contours of childhood itself, Rudolf Steiner remains something of a peculiar specter—equal parts mystic and modernist, esoteric prophet and pragmatic educator. Born in 1861 in what is now Croatia, Steiner's intellectual trajectory might seem anachronistic, a detour into spiritualism when the world was hurtling toward the silicon age. And yet, over a century later, his influence pulses quietly but insistently, especially in the realm of education.

The Waldorf school movement, inspired by his vision, has grown into a global phenomenon, educating over a million children in nearly 1,200 schools worldwide—from the bucolic hills of California to the urban sprawl of Atlanta, from a Montessori-saturated Europe to remote parts of Africa and India. These schools claim not only to teach reading and math but to nurture the whole child—intellect, body, and spirit—through art, movement, and storytelling, in a rhythm that respects developmental stages and, crucially, imagination.

If you want to understand Steiner's education philosophy today, start with what it is not: it's not about test scores or data analytics. It's about cultivating what Steiner called the "etheric body," the life force, through arts and movement, using rhythm and beauty as vehicles for learning. A child is not a vessel to be filled with facts but a seed to be nourished. In a culture where the word "performance" is practically synonymous with "value," Waldorf schools feel like an act of resistance—an embrace of mystery in an era that demands certainty.

The Netflix documentary *The Waldorf Promise* (2012) captures this ethos with a quiet reverence, following teachers and students in Brooklyn and India, revealing the movement's paradoxical blend of the old and the new. The film shot with a gentle gaze, shows classrooms free of screens filled instead with handcrafted toys, storytelling circles, and music lessons. Children learn to move their bodies in "eurythmy," a kind of spiritual dance Steiner developed to embody speech and music, a practice that seems oddly poetic against the backdrop of Tik-Tok memes and digital music. This rhythm is not just aesthetic or incidental but central to Steiner's understanding of the human being as a creature of body, soul, and spirit, all in dynamic interplay.

To talk about Steiner is to talk about anthroposophy, his system of thought which he described as "spiritual science." This was no mere spirituality of soft platitudes; Steiner saw it as rigorous, demanding a precise inner discipline akin to scientific inquiry. This work is yogic. His work touches everything from education to medicine (where biodynamic farming—Steiner's organic agriculture—has become a significant movement), to architecture, art, and philosophy.

The Goetheanum, his architectural masterpiece in Dornach, Switzerland, embodies this vision. Designed with sweeping curves and organic forms, it rejects the rigid line of modernist design and instead suggests a living organism, a space where art, spirituality, and community converge. It's a building that invites contemplation, its concrete walls seeming to breathe with light and shadow.

Biodynamic farming—born from Steiner's 1924 agriculture lectures—is perhaps his most quietly radical intervention. If industrial agriculture aims to conquer the earth, biodynamics seeks to collaborate with it. You plant by lunar cycles, stir preparations in vortexes, and treat the soil not as substrate but as soul.

This isn't a farming of nostalgia; it's an absolutely modern epistemology. And it's gaining ground. Alexander Gerber, Waldorf alumnus and CEO of Demeter Germany, has helped push biodynamics into mainstream European markets—not as a relic of esotericism, but as a serious model for sustainable agriculture. "Farming," he has said, "is a cultural activity," and in his hands, it becomes just that: the choreography of growth with conscience for the Anthropocene.

And it's not only the soil. Painters like Hilma af Klint, though predating her exposure to anthroposophy, found her spiritual language sharpened by Steiner's cosmology. Her 2018-1019 Guggenheim show, "Paintings for the Future" was a smashing critical and popular success.

Later, the healer and artist Emma Kunz would create sacred geometries so attuned to inner law they seemed less drawn than channeled. Both women were largely ignored in their time, but are now hailed as pioneers of abstraction, their work resonating with Steiner's belief that form and color were revelations of spirit.

But many contemporary artists echo Steiner—often without knowing it. Olafur Eliasson's immersive light installations, Thomas Feuerstein's biologically-driven sculptures, and the slow, reverent pacing of Terrence Malick's *The Tree of Life* all gesture toward a view of human perception as something not just reactive, but sacred. Their work is not didactic; it's devotional. And in this, it aligns with one of Steiner's central, often overlooked ideas: the aesthetic is never ornamental—it is ontological. This is the kind of idea that cuts directly against the privileging of political economy in the social and historical sciences that has led to serious blind spots across the board.

This is why it is as interesting as it is surprising how the aesthetic dimension central to Waldorf education—the handmade toys, the natural materials, the emphasis on story and myth—has seeped into broader cultural currents. In fashion and design circles, for example, a Waldorf-inspired emphasis on natural fibers and textures has quietly influenced trends away from synthetic uniformity toward something warmer, more human-scaled.

Today, this legacy is being reconsidered, adapted, and sometimes, reclaimed. In an era of teen-screen-mania and hyperconnectivity, Waldorf educators experiment with ways to maintain Steiner's core principles—particularly his skepticism of early digital exposure—while engaging a generation that is digitally native. The push and pull is palpable. Some schools have reluctantly allowed limited tech use in higher grades; others double down on the analog, presenting their campuses as refuges from the overstimulation of contemporary life.

Parents, weary of high-pressure schooling and the relentless quantification of achievement, seek Waldorf for its promise of balance and depth.

It's no coincidence that in neighborhoods marked by gentrification and cultural flux—Brooklyn, Portland, San Francisco, Berlin—Waldorf schools have found fertile ground, appealing to a demographic hungry for education that honors creativity as much as kindness and critical thinking.

But Steiner's legacy is not without features that have made it hard for people to learn about his ideas. His esoteric writings—full of challenging terms like "Spirit-Self" and "Life-Spirit"—have alienated those unfamiliar with or skeptical of occult philosophy. Critics claim that the mystical elements obscure his pedagogy and can edge into exclusionary or dogmatic territory. And while it is true that the tension between anthroposophy's spiritual aspirations and the pluralistic, secular demands of contemporary education raises difficult questions about inclusivity and evidence-based practice, these issues can be resolved by intelligent modifications that make sense for your child and for your community.

Perhaps the most enduring tension in Steiner's legacy is between the promise of a holistic human education and the realities of a world that measures success in quantifiable outcomes. The Waldorf movement's critique of early academic pressure resonates today; educators are increasingly worried about childhood anxiety and burnout. Clearly an investigation into the cause of these anxieties is warranted and will almost certainly point to social media, screen time, and neoliberal education and risk management.

Still, whether embraced or critiqued, Steiner's work insists on a vital reexamination of what it means to educate in the first place. His insistence that intellectual judgment must mature gradually—fostered not by premature critique and factual indoctrination, but by rich experience and inner development—anticipates core contemporary educational debates. How do we cultivate critical thinking without crushing imagination? How do we prepare children not only for a job but for a life? How can we stoke self-reliance and confidence without forcing kids to snap to grid? Steiner's philosophy insists that real education is ultimately a spiritual endeavor, a cultivation of the soul's capacities as much as the mind's.

In this respect, Steiner's legacy feels especially urgent now. As silicon technologies - including but not limited to artificial intelligence - accelerate, as economic, social, political, and environmental crises deepen, as democratic ideals disintegrate in the face of advanced capitalism and a global turn to the authoritarian right, and as cultural polarization grows, the questions he posed about human development, community, and the place of art and beauty in the good life have only intensified the relevance of his work. As screens increasingly narrow the senses and social media fragments attention, Steiner's vision—a call to nurture the whole human being, to slow down, to move, to create—offers a counterpoint that is radical and comforting.

Reading Steiner is like entering a labyrinth of ideas that is simultaneously arcane and accessible, visionary and grounded, historical and quintessentially contemporary. His writings, from The Philosophy of Freedom to An Introduction to Waldorf Education and Other Essays, challenge readers to look beyond materialism without dismissing reason. His influence on education and culture today is diffuse yet potent, embodied not only in schools and farms but in the subtle ways people seek meaning and connection in an increasingly fractured world.

For those willing to engage with the wonderful, compelling world Steiner offers, the reward is an invitation to imagine a different kind of future: one where education is not a race or a contest, but a journey—a dance of body, mind, and spirit.

-LC

Goetheanum (1932)

The Mission

We need to explore how the core issues facing contemporary society are related to the essential needs people have both today and in the future. This requires a serious consideration of children, and especially what good education looks like. To this end, the essay presented here attempts to offer insights and helpful suggestions on parenting and education today.

Children, Education &Thesophy

Unlocking Spiritual Wisdom for Modern Parenting and Teaching

The life of today casts doubt upon many things which humanity has inherited from its forebears—hence the countless questions that occupy our time: the social question, the women's movement, matters of education and schooling, reform of the legal system, public health, sanitation, and much more besides. We attempt to grapple with these questions in many different ways. The number of individuals who present one solution or another—each aiming to solve a particular issue or at least to contribute something meaningful toward its resolution—is vast beyond measure.

In these efforts, every imaginable shade of opinion emerges: radicalism, often bearing a revolutionary tone; moderate perspectives, which approach current conditions with respect and seek to reshape them into something new; or conservatism, which rises in resistance whenever old institutions and traditions are challenged. Alongside these primary stances, a great range of intermediary viewpoints can also be found.

Anyone capable of truly penetrating the depths of life cannot help but sense a common truth in the face of all these phenomena: the demands placed upon humanity today are repeatedly met with insufficient means. Many seek to reshape life without truly knowing it—without understanding it at its roots. Whoever wishes to make a meaningful proposal concerning the future of human life must not rest content with knowing life only on the surface. They must delve down to its very foundations.

Life resembles a plant—it holds not only what is visible to the eye but also a hidden future state within its inner depths. One who sees a plant just beginning to unfold its leaves knows that later, blossoms and fruit will emerge from the leafy stem. The seeds of these future stages are already present within the plant. Yet no one who looks only at its current form can say how these future parts will appear. Only one who understands the nature of the plant itself can make such a statement.

Human life, too, contains within itself the seeds of its own future. Yet in order to say anything meaningful about this future, one must penetrate into the hidden essence of the human being—and this is something our present age is largely unwilling to do. It concerns itself with what lies on the surface and believes it is venturing into uncertain territory whenever it attempts to approach what lies beyond outward observation. In the case of a plant, the matter is considerably simpler: we know from countless examples that similar plants have again and again produced blossoms and fruit.

But human life occurs only once, and the blossoms it is meant to bring forth in the future have never appeared before. Still, these blossoms exist in embryonic form within human life—just as surely as the flower exists within the plant that has, for now, only produced leaves.

And it is indeed possible to speak of this future—when one is willing to look beyond the surface and into the depths of human nature. The various reform ideas of our time can only bear real fruit, can only become truly practical, when they arise from such a profound inquiry into human life.

By its very nature, Theosophy is well-suited to present a practical philosophy—one that embraces the full breadth of human existence. Whether or not Theosophy itself, or what today so often goes by that name, is justified in claiming such a role is not the issue here. What matters is the essential character of Theosophy, and what, by virtue of this character, it can accomplish. It ought not to be a colorless theory that merely satisfies intellectual curiosity, nor a tool for those who, out of self-interest, seek only to elevate themselves to some higher level of personal development. Rather, it can offer something vital to the most pressing concerns of humanity today—contributing to the development of human well-being.

Naturally, if it acknowledges such a task, Theosophy must also be prepared to encounter all kinds of resistance and doubt. Radicals, moderates, and conservatives in every area of life will, without a doubt, raise objections. For at first, Theosophy may not satisfy any one group—because its insights reach far beyond the aims of any particular party or position.

Its teachings are rooted solely in a true understanding of life. Only one who understands life can truly learn from it. Such a person will not construct arbitrary plans, for they know that the laws which will govern life in the future are the same fundamental laws that govern it today. Theosophy must, by its very nature, hold a deep respect for the present state of things. Even when it finds much in the current world that calls out for improvement, it still recognizes in the present the seeds of the future.

But it also knows that everything that is in its beginnings must undergo growth and development. And so Theosophy sees, in what exists today, the potential for transformation and future flourishing. It does not fabricate grand schemes—it calls them forth from what is already present. Yet what is thus brought forth becomes, in a certain sense, a plan in itself—for it bears within it the principle of evolution.

For precisely this reason, the theosophical approach to exploring the nature of the human being must offer the most fruitful and practical means for addressing the urgent and essential questions of our time.

It is my intention to apply this approach to one such question—namely, that of education. We do not aim to advance definitive claims or deliver a scholarly dissertation, but rather to offer a simple portrayal of the nature of the child. From a thoughtful study of the developing human being, the educational perspective presented here will emerge naturally. But in order to pursue such a study in the right way, it is first necessary to contemplate the deeper, unseen aspects of human nature.

What is perceived through the senses—what the materialistic worldview considers the sole significant element of the human being, namely the physical body—constitutes according to spiritual science, only one part, one aspect of the human constitution. This physical body follows the same physical laws, and is composed of the same substances and forces, as the rest of what we call the inanimate world. Theosophy therefore holds that this physical aspect is something the human being shares with the entire mineral kingdom. It regards as the physical body only that part of the human being which is capable of combining, separating, and transforming substances according to the same laws active in the mineral world.

Yet beyond this physical body, Theosophy recognizes a second element in the makeup of the human being—what it calls the vital body or etheric body[3]

And to avoid misunderstanding: the term "etheric" as used here should not be confused with the hypothetical ether of classical physics. The meaning is entirely different and refers to what will now be described.

For some time now, it has been considered unscientific to speak of such an "etheric body." Yet this was not always the case. At the end of the eighteenth century and into the first half of the nineteenth, such language was accepted within scientific discourse. It was then widely acknowledged that matter and forces alone, as observed in minerals, could not by themselves give rise to living beings. For life to emerge, it was said, an indwelling "life force" or "vital force" must be present. This force was understood to operate in plants, animals, and human beings—just as magnetic force in a magnet produces attraction. It was held that this vital force gave rise to the phenomena of life.

In the period that followed—a time dominated by materialistic thought—this view was dismissed. It came to be asserted that living organisms arise in exactly the same way as so-called inanimate ones; that no additional forces were involved beyond those active in the mineral world. These forces, it was claimed, simply operated in a more complex fashion, giving rise to more intricate structures.

Today, only the most unyielding materialists continue to reject the notion of a vital force. Increasingly, natural philosophers and thinkers have come to recognize that something like a life-principle or vital force must indeed be acknowledged.

In this way, modern science is, to some extent, approaching the theosophical teaching concerning the vital body. Yet there remains a significant difference between the two. Contemporary science, through intellectual reflection grounded in the facts of sense perception, has begun to accept the idea of something like a vital force. But this is not the method of genuine spiritual investigation, such as Theosophy pursues, nor is it the source from which theosophical teachings arise. It cannot be emphasized often enough how Theosophy differs in this respect from the scientific outlook of our time.

Modern science regards sense perception as the foundation of all knowledge and deems anything not built on this foundation as unknowable. It draws conclusions from sensory data but dismisses anything that goes beyond these limits as lying outside the scope of human understanding. Theosophy sees such a position as analogous to that of a blind person who only acknowledges what can be touched and what can be logically inferred from touch—while disregarding the testimony of those who can see, claiming such things are beyond human capacity.

Theosophy teaches that the human being is capable of development—that through inner growth, new faculties can emerge, enabling one to access new dimensions of reality. Just as color and light surround a blind person even if he cannot perceive them, so too, Theosophy teaches, are there spiritual worlds surrounding human beings—worlds that can be perceived once the appropriate organs of perception are developed.

Just as a person who has been blind from birth might behold a completely new world after a successful operation, so can the human being—by cultivating higher faculties—gain access to entirely different worlds from those revealed by the ordinary senses. Whether or not a physical operation can restore sight depends on the condition of the physical organs; but the higher organs needed for spiritual perception exist in every human being, albeit in a latent state. Anyone can develop them—provided they bring the necessary patience, perseverance, and dedication to the methods described in my books *The Way of Initiation* and *Initiation and Its Results*.[1]

Theosophy does not speak of fixed limits to human knowledge imposed by the physical body. On the contrary, it holds that human beings are surrounded by worlds they are fully capable of perceiving—once the necessary organs are developed. Theosophy offers guidance on how to move beyond the temporary boundaries of sense-bound perception. It actively investigates the nature of the etheric, or vital body, and what will, in what follows, be called the higher aspects of human nature.

Theosophy fully acknowledges that only the physical body is accessible to the bodily senses, and that from this perspective one can arrive at something higher only through chains of reasoning or inference. But it also provides insight into how one can open up a realm in which these higher aspects of the human being appear as clearly to spiritual perception as colors and light appear to a person newly able to see.

For those who have developed these higher perceptual faculties, the etheric or vital body is not merely a theory or mental construct—it is an object of direct observation.

The human being shares this etheric body with both animals and plants. It is what enables the matter and forces of the physical body to organize themselves into the living processes of growth, reproduction, and the movement of internal fluids. The etheric body is the builder and shaper of the physical body—its indwelling force and architect.

The physical body can therefore be understood as an image or expression of this vital body. In humans, the form and size of the physical and etheric bodies are broadly similar, though they are by no means identical. In animals—and even more so in plants—the etheric body differs significantly in shape and dimension from the physical body.

The third aspect of the human being is the so-called *astral body*, or body of feeling. This is the bearer of pleasure and pain, impulse, desire, passion, and so on. A being made up only of a physical and etheric body has none of these inner experiences—none of what we rightly call *sensation*. A plant, for example, does not experience sensation. Some contemporary scientists claim that plants must have some capacity for sensation because they respond to stimuli—through movement or other reactions. But this only shows a lack of understanding about what sensation truly is.

The question is not whether a being reacts to an external stimulus, but whether that stimulus gives rise to an inner experience—such as pleasure, pain, desire, or aversion. If this be not the standard of sensation, one would be justified in asserting that blue litmus paper has a sense of feeling for certain substances, because on coming into contact with them, it turns red.[2]

The astral body—this medium of sensation and inner experience—is what the human being shares only with the animal world. It is through this third aspect that human and animal life are endowed with feeling

One must be careful not to fall into a common misunderstanding found in certain theosophical circles: the belief that the etheric body and the astral body are composed merely of finer or subtler matter than that which makes up the physical body. To think this way is to misrepresent and, in a sense, materialize these higher aspects of human nature. The etheric body is not made of matter, even of a finer kind—it is a configuration of living, active forces. Likewise, the astral body—or body of feeling—is not material, but rather a dynamic form consisting of luminous, color-filled images that shift and revolve within themselves.

The astral body differs from the physical body not only in substance but also in form and size. In the human being, it takes the shape of an elongated, oval-like structure—an aura"—in which the physical and etheric bodies are embedded. This astral body extends outward in all directions, surrounding the other two like a radiant, glowing cloud.

Now, beyond these three principles, there is a fourth that the human being does *not* share with any other earthly creature. This is the bearer of what we call the human *"I"*—the self-conscious ego. The little word *"I"*, so simple in speech, is actually unlike any other word. Anyone who reflects deeply on its nature will find themselves standing at the threshold of a real understanding of the human being.

Every other word in language can be used to refer to something external—something others can also identify in the same way. Anyone can call a table a *"table"*, or a chair a *chair"*. But *"I"* is different. No one else can use this word to refer to me—only I can do that, from within myself. You may hear the word *"I"* spoken by others, but whenever it truly applies to you, it arises only in your own inner being. To be able to say *"I"* is to declare oneself a being unto oneself—a whole world within.

Religious traditions inspired by Theosophy have long recognized the sacred character of this *"I"*. They have said: in the human *ego*, God begins to speak inwardly. In lower beings, the divine speaks only from outside, through the forms and forces of the surrounding world. But in the human *I*, the divine becomes inwardly present.

The vehicle of this highest faculty is what Theosophy calls the *"body of the ego"*, the fourth principle of the human being.[4] It is through this ego-body that the higher human soul expresses itself, and through it, the human being becomes the crown of earthly creation.

Yet in present-day humanity, the ego is not a simple or finished entity. Its nature becomes clear when we compare different human beings at various levels of development. Consider, for example, an uneducated tribesman, an average modern European, and a spiritually awakened idealist. All three are capable of saying "I", for the ego-body is present in each of them. But the way the "I" functions in each case is very different.

The uncivilized individual gives free rein to the impulses of the ego—passions, desires, instincts—much like an animal might. The more developed person allows themselves to follow certain drives but restrains or transforms others. And the idealist has cultivated not only new and nobler impulses but higher aims altogether—those that may stand in contrast to the raw desires of the lower self.

This evolution is the work of the "I" itself. It is the mission of the ego to refine, ennoble, and transform the other aspects of the human being by its own inner strength.

Under the influence of the *ego*, the lower aspects of human nature are gradually transformed—especially in those who have begun to rise above the purely external conditions into which life has placed them. Consider a human being who is just beginning to emerge from a more animal-like state: even as the *ego* first begins to shine forth within him, he still closely resembles the animal in terms of his lower principles. His etheric or vital body is simply a vehicle for the life-sustaining forces of growth and reproduction. His astral body merely expresses impulses, desires, and passions stirred by external influences.

But as this human being progresses through life—through repeated earthly lives or incarnations—struggling upward in his evolution, the *ego* gradually reshapes the other aspects of his being. Over time, the astral body becomes the medium for more refined sensations, more conscious desires and longings, both joyful and painful. The etheric or vital body, too, undergoes transformation. It becomes the carrier of habits, lasting tendencies of temperament, and the foundation of memory.

A person whose ego has not yet begun to shape the etheric body will have little true memory of lived experiences. He exists largely according to what nature has instilled in him.

The whole course of human civilization can be seen as an expression of the ego's activity upon these lower principles. This influence even reaches into the physical body. Under the *ego's* shaping power, a person's features, gestures, movements—even the entire expression of their physical form—can be altered.

We can also observe how different elements of civilization affect the different principles of the human being. The shared experiences and conventions of civilized life work primarily upon the astral body, bringing to it new forms of pleasure, discomfort, desire, and emotional tone. Deep engagement with a work of art, on the other hand, affects the etheric body. Through art, a person may gain a sense of something higher and more noble than what the ordinary senses can offer, and this subtly transforms the life-body.

One of the most powerful forces for the purification and elevation of the etheric body is *religion*. Religious impulses fulfill a profound purpose in the spiritual evolution of humanity.

What we call *conscience* is nothing other than the result of the ego's work on the etheric body over many incarnations. When a person realizes inwardly, "I must not do this," and that realization leaves a deep enough impression to shape the etheric body, then conscience begins to form.

Now, this work of the ego on the lower principles can unfold in two ways: it can be part of a broader development shared by the whole human race, or it can be the very specific inner task of the individual ego working upon itself. In the early stages of human transformation, the collective evolution of humanity plays a central role. But the more advanced stages depend entirely on the conscious activity of the individual ego.

When the ego becomes strong enough to reshape the astral body by its own strength, then the newly formed aspect of the self that arises from this work is called the *Spirit-Self* (*Geistselbst*), or, as it is known in Eastern traditions, *Manas*. This transformation essentially involves the enrichment and illumination of the inner life with higher ideas, ideals, and perceptions.

But the ego's transformative work can go still deeper—beyond the astral body—to touch the etheric body itself. This happens not just through intellectual learning, but through inner change. When a person reflects on their life, they may well say, "I've learned a great deal"—but how much harder it is to say that their *character* has changed, or their *temperament* improved, or their *memory* strengthened or weakened. Intellectual learning affects the astral body;

deeper changes—those of temperament, memory, and enduring habits—affect the etheric or vital body.

A useful image to describe this difference is that of a clock: the changes in the astral body are like the movements of the minute hand; the slower, deeper shifts in the etheric body resemble the movement of the hour hand.

When a person enters into higher or so-called *occult* training, the key task is to begin, consciously and deliberately, this deeper transformation—through the inner strength of the ego. The individual must begin to work intentionally on their own habits, their temperament, their character, their memory. And whatever portion of the etheric body the ego thus reshapes is transformed into what Theosophy calls the *Life-Spirit* (*Lebensgeist*), or in Eastern terminology, *Buddhi*.[5]

At an even higher level of development, the human being attains the capacity to transform aspects of the *physical body* itself—affecting, for example, the rhythm of the pulse or the circulation of the blood. The part of the physical body that is thus consciously and spiritually transformed is referred to as the *Spirit-Man* (*Geistesmensch*), or *Atma*.

The changes brought about in the lower aspects of human nature—not through the efforts of a single individual, but rather through collective developments of groups such as a nation, a tribe, or a family—are given particular names in Theosophy. When the astral body, or the body of feeling, is transformed by the *ego*, it becomes the *emotional soul*. The transformed etheric body becomes the *rational soul*, and the transformed physical body becomes the *self-conscious soul*. It is important not to assume that these transformations occur in strict sequence. In reality, the ego begins working on all three bodies simultaneously from the moment it first ignites in human consciousness. That said, the ego's influence generally becomes noticeable only when part of the self-conscious soul has taken shape.

From this, we can see that the human being consists of four fundamental principles:

- the *physical body*,
- the *etheric or vital body*,
- the *astral body*, or body of feeling, and
- the *ego-body*.

These give rise to the emotional soul, the rational soul, and the self-conscious soul. And beyond these lie even higher aspects of human nature—namely the *Spirit-Self* (*Manas*), *Life-Spirit* (*Buddhi*), and *Spirit-Man* (*Atma*), which are born from the gradual spiritual transformation of these foundational elements. When we speak of the roots of human faculties, it is these four primary principles that must be considered.

For any teacher or educator who seeks to nurture the human being, it is essential to understand how these principles function and evolve. One must not suppose that they develop all at once or in equal measure from birth. Rather, each matures in its own time, during distinct phases of life. A sound foundation for education must be grounded in an understanding of this law of human development.

Before physical birth, the unborn human being is enclosed by the physical body of the mother and does not et make independent contact with the outside world. It is entirely influenced and sustained by the mother's physical body. Physical birth marks the moment when the child is released from this maternal environment and becomes directly exposed to the outer world. The senses begin to awaken, and the child begins to experience the physical world firsthand, whereas before, the mother's body mediated all such contact.

From a spiritual perspective, as represented in Theosophy, this moment of birth signifies that the *physical body* has been born—but not yet the *etheric* or *vital body*. Just as the physical body was previously surrounded by the maternal womb, so too the child, until approximately age seven (the time of the second teeth), remains enveloped by etheric and astral coverings.

Only at the time of the second dentition is the etheric body "born"—that is, released to function independently. Similarly, the *astral body* remains under a kind of protective covering until puberty, at which point it too is released and becomes independent, just as the physical body was at birth and the etheric body at the change of teeth.

Thus, Theosophy speaks of *three births* in human life. Just as light and air cannot influence the physical body while it is in the womb, so too certain impressions meant for the etheric body cannot reach it directly before it is born—that is, before the second set of teeth emerges.

Prior to this, the etheric body is not fully active. Just as the fetus receives its initial development through the powers of the maternal body, the growing child—up to the age of seven—draws upon inherited and external forces that shape its etheric being.

The etheric body gradually begins to unfold its own powers during this time, and it does so in conjunction with these inherited forces. The change of teeth marks the point at which this development reaches a kind of completion: the child's own teeth, denser and more physically embedded than any other structures, emerge as symbols of this inner maturity.

After this, the etheric body becomes the primary agent of growth, now functioning on its own. Still, it remains under the influence of the as-yet-unborn astral body. Only with puberty, when the astral body also becomes free, does this next stage of development begin. The reproductive organs become fully functional, not because of inward transformation alone, but because the now independent astral body can actively engage with the world beyond.

Just as we would not expose a fetus to direct physical influences before birth, so too we must protect the child's etheric body from certain external influences until about the age of seven. And likewise, the proper development of the astral body requires that it only begin to be directly influenced by the outer world at the time of puberty.

Frequently used expressions such as "the harmonious development of all powers and talents" cannot provide a sufficient foundation for a true system of education. This is not to say such phrases are inherently wrong, but rather that they carry as little practical value as saying of a machine that all its parts should work together harmoniously. That statement may be true, but unless one understands the specific nature of the machine, one will not be able to operate it effectively.

The same applies to the art of education: it must be based on genuine insight into the human being—into the principles that make up human nature and how these principles evolve. One must know which aspect of the human being is developing at a given stage of life, and how to influence that part in a manner that is appropriate and beneficial.

There is no doubt that an educational approach as described here—one grounded in real understanding of the human being—will, for some time, only gain acceptance slowly. This is due to the prevailing mindset of our age, in which spiritual insights are still widely dismissed as the outpourings of fantasy, while commonplace slogans and surface-level ideas are mistaken for practical thinking. Nonetheless, we will now sketch an approach that many today may still see as little more than a figment of the imagination, but which, in time, will be recognized as grounded and essential truth.

At physical birth, the human body becomes subject to the physical environment of the outer world, whereas before birth it was enveloped and protected by the mother's body. What the forces and substances of the mother's body previously provided must now be replaced by the forces and elements of the surrounding physical world. Up to the time of the second dentition—around the age of seven—the human physical body has a task that is fundamentally different from those of later stages in life. During these early years, the physical organs are shaping themselves—forming specific structures and proportions. Growth continues beyond this period, but it does so on the foundation laid during these formative years.

If the shapes that formed during this time are sound and well-developed, then healthy growth can follow. But if this foundation is flawed, future development will be hindered. What a guardian neglects during these first seven years cannot be fully corrected later.

Just as nature provides the right environment for the unborn child in the womb, it becomes the responsibility of the guardian to provide the proper environment after birth. Only a fitting physical and sensory environment can influence the child in such a way that his physical organs develop into healthy, harmonious forms.

Two guiding principles capture the essential relationship between a child and their environment during this early stage of life: Imitation and Example. The Greek philosopher Aristotle once described man as the most imitative of all living beings—and this is especially true during early childhood, up until the time of the second teeth. The child imitates whatever takes place in their surroundings, and through this imitation, the physical organs take shape and direction—shapes and tendencies that often last a lifetime.

The term "physical environment" must be understood in its broadest possible sense. It includes not only the material surroundings but everything the child can perceive through their senses: every action, every gesture, every expression, every tone of voice.

All of these impressions act upon the child. This includes both moral and immoral behavior, wise or foolish actions—everything that can reach the child through the senses from all directions in space and time. All of it leaves its mark, and all of it contributes to the shaping of the physical and spiritual forces within the child.

It is not through moralizing speeches or rational instruction that a child is influenced in the manner described, but rather through the visible actions of the adults in their environment. Teaching and instruction affect only the *etheric body*, not the *physical body*. Up to the age of seven, the child's etheric body is still surrounded by a protective etheric sheath—just as the physical body, before birth, is protected within the mother's body. Whatever is meant to develop within the etheric body—ideas, habits, memory—must unfold *spontaneously*, much like the way the eyes and ears form in the womb without exposure to light.

As Jean Paul writes in his excellent educational work *Levana or Pedagogics*, a world traveler learns more from his nurse in early childhood than in all his later journeys. This statement holds profound truth—not because the child is "taught," but because the child *imitates*. Through this imitation, the physical organs of the child take shape. A healthy capacity for seeing, for instance, arises when a child is surrounded by harmonious colors and lighting conditions.

In a similar way, the physical basis for a sound moral life is laid in the brain and circulatory system when the child observes moral behavior in their surroundings. If, up to the age of seven, the child continually sees foolish actions, then the brain is likely to develop in such a way that it is only capable of foolishness in later life.

Just as the hand muscles grow strong through use, so too do the brain and other organs of the physical body develop correctly when they are engaged by the appropriate environmental impressions. One example illustrates this well: a doll can be made from a piece of cloth, with corners twisted to represent arms and legs, a knot for a head, and features drawn with ink—or one might buy a so-called "beautiful" doll, with lifelike hair and painted cheeks. The latter, though considered attractive by many, is actually quite damaging. It risks spoiling the child's sense of beauty for life.

When a child plays with the simple cloth doll, they must actively *imagine* the figure it represents. This imaginative effort stimulates the brain's development, just as physical effort strengthens the muscles. But when a ready-made, lifelike doll is given, the brain has no creative work to do—it becomes passive, stunted, dried up instead of growing.

If people could observe the way the brain develops—much like an occultist is able to—many would choose playthings that truly support the development of the child's inner capacities. Toys made up only of rigid, geometric forms have a deadening effect. By contrast, toys that suggest movement, life, and action support healthy brain growth.

Our materialistic era offers few truly good toys. But one example from traditional culture remains: a simple toy showing two wooden figures hammering together, often still found in rural areas. Another excellent example is a picture book with figures that move when pulled by strings. These kinds of toys allow the child to animate static images, fostering internal activity. From this inner activity, the child's organs take on the right shapes and functions.

Of course, these examples only hint at a broader picture. In the future, *spiritual science* will be called upon to offer guidance in these matters in a more detailed and individualized way. It is not an abstract theory, but a body of living knowledge, fully capable of giving direction in practical life.

Here is another example: from the perspective of spiritual science, a child who is excitable and nervous must be treated differently from one who is lethargic and passive. Everything matters—the colors of the room, the design of their surroundings, even the color of the clothes they wear. Without spiritual insight, we often make the wrong choices. A materialistic mindset may easily suggest exactly the opposite of what is needed.

For instance, an overly excitable child should be dressed in red or reddish-yellow clothing, and surrounded by similar warm tones. A more passive child should be surrounded by blue or bluish-green. This is because colors produce their complementary opposites within the human being. Red stimulates the inner perception of green; blue, of orange-yellow. You can observe this by staring at a colored surface and then quickly looking at a white background—the complementary color will appear. These complementary hues are generated by the child's physical organs and, in turn, influence internal bodily functions.

Thus, surrounding an excitable child with red encourages an internal green response. This green has a calming effect, promoting balance and composure. The body, through this complementary activity, learns to temper its excitability.

One rule must always be kept in mind during this stage of life: the physical body itself must create the standard of what is suitable for it. It does this through the development of corresponding desires. In general, a healthy physical body desires only what is good for it. So, when considering the physical body of a growing child, careful attention should be paid to what the healthy desires, cravings, and pleasures actually seek. Joy and pleasure are the forces that best help the physical organs form and develop.

A serious mistake can be made by failing to place the child in the right physical conditions in its environment. This is especially important regarding the instinct of nourishment. A child can be overfed in such a way that healthy instincts for food are lost entirely. But with correct feeding, these instincts can be preserved so well that the child will naturally ask—even for something as simple as a glass of water—for what is truly good for them, and will reject anything harmful. When occult science is applied to create an educational system, it will be able to specify, down to particular foods and table delicacies, everything that needs to be considered here. This is a practical teaching relevant to life, not a vague or colorless theory—as is sometimes mistakenly thought, even by some Theosophists today.

Among the forces that shape the physical organs, joy amid the surroundings must be included. Let the guardian be cheerful in countenance, and above all, let there be genuine—not artificial—love. Such love, flowing warmly through the physical environment, truly nurtures and incubates the development of the physical organs.

When the child is surrounded by such an atmosphere of love and has healthy models to imitate, the child is in the right element. Special care should be taken to ensure that nothing occurs in the child's environment that they should not copy.

Nothing should be done that would force the guardian to say, "You must not do that." We can see how the child imitates by observing how it can copy written letters long before understanding their meaning. Indeed, it is advisable for the child to copy letters first and only later learn their significance. This is because imitation belongs primarily to the developing physical body, while the mind corresponds to the etheric body, which should only be influenced after the time of the second teeth, when its outer etheric covering is shed. Especially during these years, learning speech through imitation is crucial, as children learn best by hearing. All rules and artificial teaching at this stage are of little use.

In early childhood, educational tools such as children's songs should make as beautiful a rhythmic impression on the senses as possible. The importance lies more in the beauty of the sound than in the meaning. The more invigorating the effect upon the eyes and ears, the better. The power of building the organs through dancing movements, especially when combined with musical rhythm, must not be underestimated.

With the change of teeth, the etheric body sheds its outer covering, and then the time begins when the etheric body may be trained from outside influences. It is important to understand what can influence the etheric body in this way. The growth and transformation of the etheric body correspond to the development of affections, habits, conscience, character, memory, and temperament. The etheric body can be influenced through pictures, examples, and carefully guided use of imagination.

Just as a child before age seven needs physical models to imitate, so too, between the time of the second teeth and puberty, everything in the child's environment should have an inner meaning and value toward which the child can direct attention. All that stimulates thought, all that works through imagery and metaphor, has its proper place during this period.

The etheric body develops its strength when a well-guided imagination focuses on living images and parables, or on ideas addressed to the spirit, rather than on abstract concepts. Concrete—not abstract—ideas that are spiritually, rather than materially, concrete, are what truly influence the growing etheric body. Thus, during these years, education from a spiritual perspective is essential.

It is very important that the youth be surrounded by guardians who themselves are strong personalities, whose viewpoints can awaken the desired intellectual and moral powers within him.

Just as "imitation" and "example" are the key words for educating children in their early years, so too are "hero-worship" and "authority" the guiding principles for this later stage. Natural, not forced, authority must provide the spiritual framework by which the youth develops conscience, habits, and character, regulates temperament, and forms his own view of the world. The poet's beautiful words—"Everyone must choose his own hero, in whose steps he may find the way to Olympus"—capture this perfectly for this stage of life.

Veneration and reverence are forces that help the etheric body grow in the right way. A young person who cannot look up to anyone with deep reverence during this period will suffer for it throughout life. Without this veneration, the vital forces of the etheric body become blocked. Imagine this: a boy of eight is told about a highly respected person. Everything he hears fills him with holy awe. When the day comes to meet this honored person, he is overcome with profound reverence as the doorbell rings. These beautiful feelings are lifelong treasures. A fortunate person is one who, not just during happy moments but always, can look up to his teachers and mentors as natural authorities.

Alongside these living authorities—embodiments of moral and intellectual strength—there must be spiritual authorities. Great historical figures and stories of exemplary men and women help shape conscience and intellectual leanings far more effectively than abstract moral truths, which only truly take hold after puberty, when the astral body sheds its outer covering.[6]

Teaching history, especially, should be guided by this understanding. Before the second teeth appear, stories and fairy tales told to children should focus on joy, entertainment, and pleasure. After this time, care must be taken in choosing what is shared so that the young person's soul is presented with images of life that he can beneficially imitate. It's important to remember that negative habits can be driven out by showing correspondingly repulsive images. Warnings alone do little good, but if the living image of a bad person is shown to the youth, along with an explanation of where such behavior leads, much can be done to eradicate those tendencies.

Always keep in mind that it is not abstract ideas that influence the developing etheric body, but vivid, living pictures of spiritual clarity. And these must be used with the greatest sensitivity—otherwise, the opposite of what is intended may occur. With stories, how they are told is crucial; reading a tale silently can never replace the power of a spoken narration.

Between the time of the second teeth and puberty, symbolic or spiritually pictorial teaching should be approached in a special way. At this stage, young people need to learn the secrets of nature and the laws of life primarily through symbols and allegories—not through dry, intellectual explanations. These allegories should reach the soul so that the underlying law and order of existence is sensed and intuited, rather than just understood intellectually. The motto "all things transient are only symbols" should guide education during this period.

It is very important for a person to first receive the secrets of nature as allegories before encountering them later as natural laws or abstract ideas. For example, if one wants to explain the immortality of the soul and its departure from the body after death, one might compare it to a butterfly emerging from a chrysalis. Just as the butterfly leaves its chrysalis, so the soul leaves the body. Without such an image, the abstract idea is much harder to grasp fully.

This kind of comparison speaks not just to the intellect but to the entire soul, engaging feelings and sensations. After this experience, the youth will approach intellectual concepts with a different, deeper mindset. Anyone who cannot

irst approach life's mysteries with such feeling is truly un-
ortunate.

Teachers need to have suitable similes for all natural laws
and world secrets. Occult science enriches this process im-
mensely. Someone trying to use materialistic or purely intel-
ectual similes will often fail to impress young people. For
imiles to be effective, the teacher must first have deeply un-
lerstood and believed in them themselves. This conviction
llows a subtle spiritual influence to flow from teacher to
tudent. Without genuine belief in the similes, the teacher
annot inspire or convince.

True influence comes when the teacher believes in the
imiles as if they were realities. This requires a mystical
lisposition and that the similes arise from occult science.
he real occultist does not hesitate to use the soul's depar-
ure from the body and the butterfly's emergence from the
hrysalis as parallel truths because he knows them from ex-
•erience. His belief flows naturally and powerfully to the
stener, inspiring conviction. This direct "life-stream" from
eacher to pupil requires that the teacher's words be filled
vith warmth, feeling, and the true perspective of occult wis-
om.

Occult science reveals a magnificent vision of education.
)nce education draws from this life-source, it gains pro-
ound vitality and leaves behind the aimless wandering com-
10n in this field. Educational methods that do not
ontinually renew themselves from such deep roots become
ried up and dead. Occult science provides fitting simi-
•s—not inventions of the mind, but truths drawn from the

very essence of existence and laid down by the forces of creation.

Therefore, occult science must form the foundation of any genuine system of education.

A key power of the soul that deserves special attention during this developmental period is memory. The cultivation of memory is closely connected to the transformation of the etheric body. This is because between the arrival of the second teeth and puberty, the etheric body becomes free, making this the ideal time for memory development to be nurtured from the outside. If this opportunity is neglected, the memory will be permanently weaker than it could have been—what is lost at this stage cannot be recovered later.

An intellectual and materialistic mindset often leads to mistakes here. Education systems based on this way of thinking tend to distrust simple memory training. They work hard to prevent young people from mechanically absorbing information they don't fully understand.

Materialistic thinkers usually believe that understanding only comes through abstract intellectual ideas, and it's hard for them to accept that other inner powers—such as feeling and emotions—are just as vital to true comprehension as intellect itself.

It is not merely a figure of speech to say that one can understand with feelings, emotions, and intuition as well as with the intellect. Ideas are just one way to grasp the world. Yet materialists treat intellectual concepts as the only valid means of understanding. Many people, even those who claim to hold spiritual or idealistic views, often still have a materialistic soul attitude because they rely solely on intellect to understand the world. The intellect, after all, is primarily the soul's tool for comprehending material things.

On the deeper foundations of understanding, let's quote from the excellent educational book by Jean Paul, which contains many valuable insights but is not given the attention it deserves. The passage says:

"Do not fear unintelligibility, even if whole sentences are unclear; your expression and eager desire to understand will clarify half the meaning, and in time, the other half as well. For children, like speakers of foreign languages, much of communication is conveyed by tone and manner. Remember that children understand their language as little as we understand Greek before learning it. Trust time and association to bring meaning. A five-year-old might grasp words like 'yet,' 'truly,' 'on the contrary,' or 'of course,' but to define these, ask the father! The little word 'but' reveals a small philosopher. If an eight-year-old child can be understood by a three-year-old, why limit your language to the younger child's level? Speak always several years ahead, as geniuses in books speak to us centuries ahead. Speak to a one-year-old as if it were two, to a two-year-old as if it were six—growth differences decrease as years pass.

Generally, too much credit for learning is given to the teacher. Remember that the child already possesses half his world internally—his moral and metaphysical ideas—so language made only of concrete images cannot teach spiritual ideas but can only ignite them. The joy and confidence you bring when speaking to children should seem to come from themselves. We can learn speech from children as they learn from us, through bold and vivid word-painting—such as children saying 'leg-fish' for otter, 'pig-iron' for a fork used to eat bacon, or 'air-mouse' (a charming alternative to our word 'bat')."

This passage acknowledges that Jean Paul's words originally refer to understanding before intellectual comprehension, but they also hold important lessons for memory development. Just as a child learns to speak without intellectual knowledge of grammar rules, so too should a youth learn and memorize facts before fully understanding them. What is first learned mechanically by memory can later be grasped intellectually—much like learning language rules after speaking fluently.

The common criticism against rote learning—that it is mechanical and mindless—is a materialistic prejudice. For example, a youth only needs to learn a few multiplication rules by example, then memorize the multiplication table by heart, ideally using natural methods like finger counting rather than abacuses. This respects the child's developmental nature.

However, a mistake is to demand too much intellectual effort before puberty. Since the intellect matures around puberty, it should not be overloaded earlier. Instead, the young person should accumulate knowledge through memory, and only later engage with it intellectually. In other words, one should not merely remember what one understands, but rather come to understand what one has already memorized—just as children learn to speak before mastering grammar.

This principle applies broadly: first, memorize historical events, then understand their meaning; first, learn geographical facts, then grasp their relationships. Comprehension through ideas is best built on the foundation of stored memories. The richer the memory before intellectual understanding, the better.

This applies only to this developmental period. Later in life, the reverse may be true—understanding first, then memorization—depending on the individual's nature. But during childhood and early youth, the spirit must not be overwhelmed by intellectual ideas.

Similarly, teaching that relies solely on sense objects reflects a materialistic outlook. Every idea at this age must be spiritualized. For example, a seed is not just a physical object but a symbol of the invisible life within it. This spiritual reality must be felt through perception, imagination, and feeling, not just observed with the senses.

Far from weakening sensory perception, this approach enriches it. Truth exists in both spirit and matter, and true observation requires both physical and spiritual faculties. An education focused only on physical objects neglects this deeper reality and thus impairs both body and soul.

Materialists may dismiss these ideas as fanciful, just as occult science seems fantastic to them. Nonetheless, a truly practical education cannot come from materialistic views, no matter how "practical" they seem. Overcoming resistance to occult teachings in education is expected since these truths are unfamiliar to many, but if true, they will eventually become part of culture.

Only when teachers are convinced that these spiritual and memory-based methods are the only effective ways to influence young people can they properly nurture each child's individual soul powers—thinking, feeling, and willing—and guide the etheric body, which between the arrival of the second teeth and puberty is especially receptive to external shaping.

The foundation for a strong and healthy will can be established during the first seven years through proper education. The will depends on the fully developed physical body, which from the time of the second teething is supported and strengthened by the developing etheric body. The etheric body gains strength most through impressions that connect a person to the eternal Universe—namely, through profound religious experiences. Without such experiences, the will and character remain unstable and unhealthy. A well-formed will comes from feeling intimately connected to a Supreme Spirit and the whole world.

The emotional nature is nurtured through allegories, vivid sense-pictures, and especially through exposure to figures of strong character—whether from history or other sources. A deep engagement with nature's mysteries and beauty is also essential to build the emotional world.

Cultivating a sense of beauty, especially through the arts, is crucial. Music, in particular, imparts rhythm to the etheric body, enabling a person to perceive the hidden rhythms of life. A young person who misses this musical cultivation loses access to a vital dimension of the Universe. Other arts—architecture, sculpture, design, harmony of colors—must also be included in education. Even under limited circumstances, much can be done if the teacher has a true sense for these arts.

From the cultivation of beauty and art arise joy, love of life, and strength to work. These qualities enrich all human relationships, making them nobler and more beautiful. The moral sense, developed by life examples and authorities, gains stability when the good is recognized as beautiful and the bad as ugly through this cultivated sense of beauty.

Thought, in its pure form as an inner life of refined ideas, must during this period be kept in the background. It should develop spontaneously, as it were, free from external influence, while the soul is nourished through similes and images that represent life and the mysteries of nature. Thus, amid the other experiences of the soul between the seventh year and puberty, thought must grow and the capacity for judgment mature, so that after a successful puberty the individual becomes capable of forming independent opinions on matters of life and knowledge. Indeed, the less one directly exercises the critical faculty at this stage, and the more one fosters it indirectly through the development of other spiritual powers, the better it will be for the person's entire future life.

Occult science establishes principles not only for the spiritual aspects of education but for the purely physical as well. For example, consider gymnastics and children's games. Just as love and joy must suffuse the environment in early childhood, so too must the developing etheric body be taught to genuinely experience through physical exercise a sense of its own expansion and ever-growing strength. Gymnastic exercises, for instance, should be carried out so that with every movement, with every step, the child feels inwardly: "I sense increasing power within me." This feeling should manifest as a healthy delight, a sensation of pleasure.

To design such exercises in this way requires more than mere intellectual knowledge of human anatomy and physiology. It demands a close, intuitive, and sympathetic understanding of how joy and comfort relate to bodily postures and movements. The person who devises these exercises must personally experience how one movement or posture of the limbs produces a pleasant, comfortable sensation while another causes a loss of strength, and so forth.

The conviction that gymnastics and bodily exercises can be developed along these lines can only be imparted to the educator through occult science, or at the very least, by a mind sympathetic to such ideas. One does not even need to possess the ability to see into the spiritual worlds—only the willingness to apply in life what occultism has revealed.

If especially in such practical areas of education occult knowledge were applied, all the pointless debates about whether this knowledge needs further proof would immediately end. For to those who correctly apply it, this knowledge proves itself through life itself, by making them healthy and strong. In this way, one would deeply perceive its truth in practice, and would find this a far better proof than any so-called "logical" or "scientific" arguments. Spiritual truths are best recognized by their fruits, not by a supposed proof however scientific it may claim to be, for such proofs are little more than intellectual skirmishes.

At puberty, the astral body is first born. With the free outward development that follows, everything revealed through the world of external perceptions, one's judgment and unfettered understanding will rush inward upon the soul. It has already been noted that these faculties of the soul, until now uninfluenced from within, ought to be developed through the proper management of educational methods, just as the eyes and ears develop unconsciously in the womb. But with puberty, the time has come when the person is ready to form their own judgment concerning what they have learned so far.

No greater harm can be done to anyone than to awaken their independent judgment too early. One should only judge once they have already gathered the necessary qualifications for judging and comparing. If independent opinions are formed prematurely, they will lack a solid foundation. All forms of one-sidedness in life, all narrow "confessions of faith" based on mere fragments of knowledge, and the urge to judge human concepts approved over long ages rest on precisely such educational mistakes.

Before one is qualified to think critically, one must place before oneself, as a caution, what others have thought. There is no sound thinking that has not been preceded by a solid perception of truth supported by clear authority. If one wishes to follow these educational principles, one must not allow young people to fancy themselves able to judge too early.

By avoiding this, one preserves their ability to allow life to influence them from every side, without prejudice. For every premature judgment, not based on the precious foundation of spiritual treasures, becomes a stumbling block in the path of life. Once a judgment is pronounced on any subject, the one who makes it will always be influenced by having done so; they will no longer regard an experience as they might have if no opinion had been formed and entwined with that subject.

Young people should possess the disposition first to learn and only then to judge. What the intellect has to say about a subject should only be expressed once all other soul powers have spoken; before that, the intellect should act only as a mediator. It should simply grasp what is seen and felt, apprehending it as it is, without allowing premature judgment to take hold of the matter. Therefore, the youth should be shielded from all theories about a subject before the age mentioned above, and it must be especially emphasized that they should face life experiences openly, admitting them fully into their soul.

A growing individual can certainly be introduced to what others have thought about this or that, but premature judgments should be avoided. Opinions should be received with feeling, without immediately deciding for one side or the other, without attaching to a party, but thinking as one listens: "One says this, another says that." Above all, a great deal of tact is required from teachers and guardians in cultivating this sense, and occult knowledge is precisely designed to provide such tact.

Only a few aspects of education in the light of Occultism have been developed here, but the aim has been merely to hint at the civilizational problems this philosophy must address. Whether it can succeed depends on whether the inclination toward this way of thinking broadens ever further. For this to happen, two things are necessary: first, that people abandon their prejudice against Occultism.

Those who truly engage with it will soon see that it is not the fanciful nonsense many today imagine. This is not a reproach, for everything offered as education today must at first lead to the view that occultists are mere dreamers. On the surface, no other view seems possible, for there appears to be complete opposition between Occult Science or Theosophy and the principles that present-day culture offers as foundations for a healthy worldview.

Only deeper reflection reveals how utterly the current views must fail without the principles of occult science—how indeed, they themselves call out for these principles and ultimately cannot exist without them. The second necessity concerns the sound development of Theosophy itself. Life will only welcome Theosophy if within theosophical circles it is made clear that it is essential to bring these teachings to practical fruition in all areas of life, not merely to theorize about them. Otherwise, people will continue to regard Theosophy as a sectarian curiosity fit only for fanatic enthusiasts. But if it performs genuinely positive spiritual work, the theosophical movement cannot, in the long run, be denied intelligent consideration.

Eurythmische Tänzerinnen 1926, Anton Josef Trčka

Footnotes

A. Eurythmy can be performed with spoken word—through recitation or dramatic speech—and with instrumental music. Yet it's essential to understand that Eurythmy is not dancing in any conventional sense. It is, rather, music translated into movement. The distinction between Eurythmy and dancing is fundamental. Still, it's a distinction easily overlooked by audiences, especially in stage performances, likely because Eurythmy uses the moving human body as its expressive instrument. Some observers, unfamiliar with its underlying principles, have misread this. But what defines Tone-Eurythmy—the practice of making music visible through movement, accompanied by instrumental sound—is precisely its difference from dance. Tone-Eurythmy is not dance. It is embodied singing, choreographed response to musical tone and rhythm, where movement becomes a form of listening made visible. Today, contemporary ensembles like the Eurythmy Spring Valley Ensemble explore this evolving art form. Their performances work the interplay of movement and music, offering audiences a living experience of Eurythmy's unique expressive power.

Children, Education & Theosophy

1. *"The Way of Initiation,"* or *How to Attain Knowledge of the Higher Worlds,* by Rudolph Steiner, Ph.D., contains

a Foreword by Annie Besant, and some biographical notes on the author by Edouard Schuré. 2nd edition, 237 pages, clothbound. Or try *"Initiation and its Results,"* a sequel to *"The Way of Initiation."* second edition.

2. This distinction is important because current ideas on the subject tend to be rather unclear. The difference between plants and creatures endowed with sensation is often overlooked, since the essential nature of sensibility is not clearly defined. When a being (or an object) responds to an external stimulus by any effect at all, it is inaccurate to conclude that the impression has been truly felt. To justify this conclusion, the impression must be experienced inwardly—meaning the external stimulus must produce some kind of internal reflection. The great advances of natural science, which a true Theosophist must genuinely admire, have unfortunately muddled our abstract vocabulary. Some biologists are unaware of what true sensibility entails, and thus mistakenly attribute it to beings that lack it. The sensibility understood by these biologists can indeed be attributed to organisms devoid of true feeling. But the sensibility meant by Theosophy is an entirely different quality.

3. A distinction must be drawn between the conscious inner life of the astral body and the perception of this life by external clairvoyant observation. Here, the latter—perception by a trained clairvoyant—is intended.

4. The reader should not object to the technical term "Body of the ego," because it does not refer to gross physical matter. However, since occult science must use ordinary language, the words applied in Theosophy should from the start be understood in a spiritual sense.

5. The terms "Spirit-Self," "Life-Spirit," and "Spirit-Man" need not confuse the reader; they refer to those transformations of our grosser bodies which are the results of conscious effort and pure aspirations. In other words, they form the Higher Trinity, called in Eastern terminology: Manas, Buddhi, and Atma, respectively.

6. Were these statements misunderstood, one may object that a child before cutting its second teeth is not without memory, and that before puberty, it already possesses the inherent faculties of the astral body. It must not be forgotten that the etheric and astral bodies exist from the moment of physical birth, although surrounded by the protective shell described earlier. It is precisely this envelope protecting the etheric body that allows for remarkably good memory even before the second teeth appear. The presence of physical eyes in the embryo, hidden in the mother's womb, is similar. Just as the physical eyes, shielded from all external influence, do not owe their development to sunlight, so too education from outside should not intervene in memory training before the second teeth appear. Quite the opposite: spontaneous growth of memory will be noticeable, provided there is nourishment for

it and no attempt is made to train it by external methods. This observation applies equally to the qualities of the astral body before puberty. Their training should be provided for, but with the understanding that this body is still enclosed in a protective shell. There is a fundamental difference between caring for the developing seeds within the astral body before puberty and exposing the freed astral body after puberty to all it can assimilate in the outer world, without this shell. This distinction is subtle, but without careful consideration of it, the full meaning of education cannot be understood.

Notes

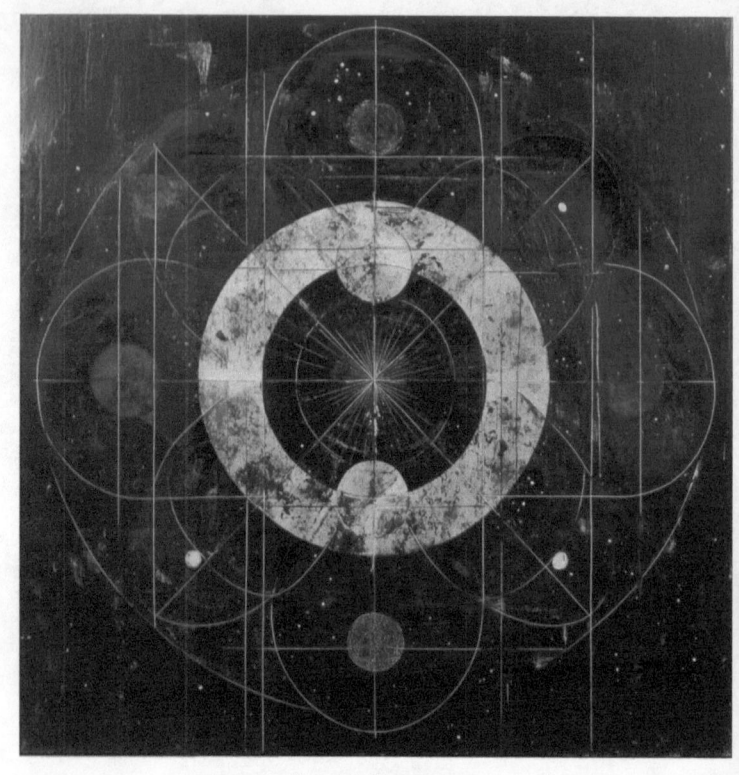

Sacred Geometry

DDP

Decatur Dixon of Shelby, North Carolina is widely read and widely traveled. While he has sampled every dish and libation placed in front of him and fishes at least once a week, his favorite activity is reading. Every genre, every era. This book is the fifth in a curated series of favorites. Decatur Dixon Publishing specializes in illustrated classics as well as poetry, philosophy, and writing that sits between genres of all stripes. Lula Crowder is a bohemian of the highest order. Classically trained, she has offered curated shows as well as her own work in the salons of New York, San Francisco, Savannah, and elsewhere. Her book illustrations are best known for appearing in manilla envelopes tucked into library editions and borrowed collections as gifts to future readers.

Visit us at DecaturDixonPress.com